Abinaya Rajasekaran, Ashok Kumar

User Preference Based Environment Provisioning in Cloud

GRIN Publishing

Bibliographic information published by the German National Library:

The German National Library lists this publication in the National Bibliography; detailed bibliographic data are available on the Internet at http://dnb.dnb.de .

Imprint:

Copyright © 2015 GRIN Verlag GmbH
Print and binding: Books on Demand GmbH, Norderstedt Germany
ISBN: 978-3-656-93840-8

This book at GRIN:

http://www.grin.com/en/e-book/295645/user-preference-based-environment-provi-sioning-in-cloud

GRIN - Your knowledge has value

Since its foundation in 1998, GRIN has specialized in publishing academic texts by students, college teachers and other academics as e-book and printed book. The website www.grin.com is an ideal platform for presenting term papers, final papers, scientific essays, dissertations and specialist books.

Visit us on the internet:

http://www.grin.com/

http://www.facebook.com/grincom

http://www.twitter.com/grin_com

User Preference based Environment provisioning in cloud

[1]Abinaya Rajasekaran, Student of Sathyabama University, Chennai-600119,Tamil Nadu,India.
[2]Ashok kumar, Department of Computer Science and Engineering, Sathyabama University,Chennai-6000119 Tamil Nadu,India.

Abstract : To deploy an application, a single cloud service is not enough. Different cloud services are available, but users should provide compositions and configurations, to deliver their solutions. But identifying, analyzing the compatibility, selecting and application deployment of the above, is a complex process. It is difficult for the users to find the compatible composition for their requirement. Main Challenge is to create a self configuring application framework which will deploy the application automatically.The selection of this composition is a challenging task and also ranking system is not available to compare and choose, selecting the server type and also software solution for their deployment. Therefore we suggests Cloud service composition for naïve users based on their preferences Thus users need not be forced to assign exact weights for their preferences.

The main aim of this project is check the compatibility of the Web Application with the Cloud Service composition and to build a Virtual Machine (Instance) for Deployment and various Preferences of Users (User Input).

- User with less technical knowledge can handle the cloud server and deploy their application on cloud.

- Cost will be considered as important component to configure the server on cloud.

Keywords: Environment provisioning, IAAS, Cloud, Pay as you use, Technical challenges, Application deployment on cloud environemnt.

I.INTRODUCTION

Cloud Computing is defined as any service like server, storage, database, software, product hosted on Internet. so that everyone can use these services with Internet connection and so that there will not be any location constrains. Instead of investing more on computing infrastructures, companies started to consume computing as service.

Benefits of Cloud Computing:

• Elasticity: Auto scaling is biggest benefit since we can scale up and scale down the computing services when ever required. Companies can configure the environment as per their requirement.
• Pay per use: User will pay only for the services they use, by which we can reduce the cost spend on infrastructures.

Application deployment in cloud has been increasing nowadays since the user need not concentrate much on the infrastructure needed for the application deployment. For they can setup their infrastructure in cloud and pay based on demand. This makes cloud services indispensable and reduces the infrastructure management effort. The management effort includes hardware upgrade, patching, maintenance.

Cloud computing is classified as private cloud, public cloud and hybrid cloud. Type of cloud can be choosed as per the requirment. Private cloud is creating a cloud environment or service for internal user in an organization. Public cloud is using the cloud environment over internet by using third party cloud services. Hybrid cloud include both Public and private cloud service.

Cloud computing are classified to below categories as per their service: Infrastructure as a service, Platform as a service and software as a service.

Cloud services are being used in all the business because of its various offerings provided by its vendors. Cloud services includes servers, data center, database, shared storage, email sevices, queue service, sms services and so on. Because of its wide range of service it grabbed wide range of business in various fields like banking, insurance, commercial, social, media, research fields. Biggest advantage of cloud computing is we can use services from anywhere with good internet connection, pay for what we use, services are provided and managed by vendors we can customize and use as per our business requirement

1

II. RELATED WORKS

Cloud services includes virtual machine and application which works in compatible with each other. Cloud computing is getting fame day by day but it also a make it tough for non-expert users with less knowledge on to deploy their services faultlessly.[6] When it comes to IAAS it involves lot of architectural, configuration and security details to be selected for launching a server in cloud environment. Which makes it a big challenge for users to prefer cloud services. Adavntage of cloud services is cost and it might become a disadvantage when it is not utilized properly.[1] illustrated the provisioning of virtual machines based on the user requested time and cost and also autoscaling of the same based on the utilization of the provisioned instances. [1] have presented a coordinated dynamic resource provisioning and scheduling approach that is able to maximize number of application execution within their deadlines and budget. [3] new method of allocating resource with minimum wastage and providing maximum profit in resource allocation model, users send service request or task to be executed on cloud environment.[9] analysed and provided an abstract on the problem related to resource allocation. performs massively parallel search to find a solution that meets all the specified objectives.[2] provides details on configuring virtual machines with all the composition details on private cloud environment. [11] analyzed various resource provisioning techniques identified and the merits and demerits of the same. One of the techniques they have suggested is "Dynamic provisioning in multi-tenant service". Here Adaptive power-aware virtual machine provisioner is used for provisioning dynamically from the resource pool.[4] selection of the resourses plays main role in environment provisioning the resourses are key for application deployment. From the list of available resourses priority based and preference based algorithm will select the resourses for environment provisioning in cloud. Next step will be to deploy the appplication automatically on the server selected [20]. Select the right image from the list based on the user input and then application will be deployed on the server and then user willl be able to access their application on the cloud environment.

III. SYSTEM ANALYSIS

The essential thought behind the proposed framework is to use the cloud service more cost effeciently and also let non technical user to use the cloud environment. Deploying a web application in cloud is a complex task for the naïve user.Using this application user can build their own instance based on their requirements. Web applications dependencies are available, the only thing is user has to select their web application dependencies based on his/her preferences. Since cloud service is upcoming field in market we are able to see less techincal support available in market, this kind of framework will let the business choose cloud option with out much fear on support on technology to deploy the application on cloud. we suggest a solution which will simplify using cloud service for the users, based on their preferences like RAM, Storage, time within the Project cost.

Users can create a cloud environment for the cost they specify instead of going for paying for the infrastructure they provide. Which will largely reduce the cost and also fear of the users to go for cloud infrastructure. Biggest Challenge in creating a framework for application deployment is to create a self configuring environment and deploy the application on it.Selection of this composition is a complex task and also we suggest ranking system to priorties the best option available.

ARCHITECTURE DIAGRAM:

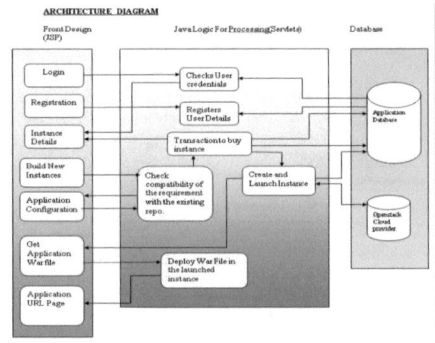

Figure 1: Architectural representation of the framework

Figure [1] Architecture of the framework represent three layers in which user interface layer will be user friendly which will make user comfortable with accessing cloud environment. Basic details like cost, server infra details and application complexity details will be optained from user and the same will be used in analyzing and processing the request.the java layer will include all the business validation and algorithm analysis to rank the best instance for the user input.once the user confirms the instance then it will be activated and made available for requester to access it. Then dynamic deployment will be facilitated by which user will also be able to deploy their application on cloud environment.

User preference based ranking algorithm

Userinput : details entered by user includes budget,os,db,webserver.
Appweight :complexity of the application as entered by user.
Imageconf: list of image and configuration details in cloud repository.
Case 1 : user enter cost & configuration details

Check: Compare user input and available image
    If (image match){
        If(morethan one image){
            Rank the image with lowest cost as rank1 and others with the subsequent ranks based on cost.
        }else{
            Rank the available image as rank1 and suggest the user.
        }
    }else{
        User needs to try different compination of input.
    }
Case 2: user enter only cost
Check: compare the user cost and available image cost.
If (image match){
    If(morethan one image){
        Rank the image with lowest cost as rank1 and others with the subsequent ranks based on cost.
    }else{
        Rank the available image as rank1 and suggest the user.
    }
}else{
    User needs to try different compination of input.
}

IV. IMPLEMENTATION

Aim of this proposal is to create an environment to deploy application which is auto configuring and with various components. Considering the deployment requirements of a web application, it should include application servers, security frameworks (e.g. firewall), web servers, database storage and hard disk storage devices.

Creating a complex application environment setup is costly, complex and error prone. Virtual appliances on cloud, provides solution to these problems. Cloud service providers create and configure servers and environments with required configuration details like operation system, software configurations as per user requirement. Therefore we are proposing a framework which provision an environment for the end user to host their application in cloud. We are getting the user requirements and validating the same. We then check whether it is feasible to provide the infrastructure services for the customer's web application. We are trying to provide an infrastructure within the customer expectation like Project cost and launch virtual instance to host the customer's web application

To create a cloud repository, i.e. resource pool based on which the users requirement will be compared, we are using Openstack as a cloud service provider. First we have virtualized our environment using Virtual Box and launched Ubuntu image over it. In the installed Ubuntu image, we have installed Openstack. Openstack has different components needed to bring up and manage virtual instances on a physical hardware. Using Openstack, we are provisioning the virtual instances based on the user requirements and we are deploying the web application mentioned by the user. The compatibility algorithm that we suggest compares the user requirement with the resources available in resource pool. If sufficient resources available, it checks for the application dependencies and checks for the same in the resource pool. If all the need cloud services are available, it will launch an instance using the Openstack API.

The customer's web application will then be deployed in the launched virtual instances. We present an application URL to the customer to access the application. Thus the customer's application can be easily deployed and managed in a private cloud environment using Openstack.

a) User will login to the system and get the give their requirement with the option available we here make the system will simple option to the

3

user so that they will not face any techinical difficulty in accessing the application. Figure [2].

b) Priority and user preference based algorithm will analyse user input and compare the existing options provide ranking and give the user best Instance available in the cloud repository.

c) Cloud reposiroty will have collection of images with various combination.with api's selected insatance will be launched and application will also be deployed on the server.

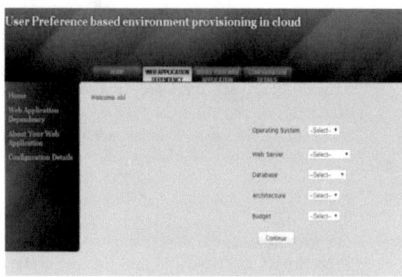

Figure 2. User Interface to get input from user – cost and configuration details

PERFORMANCE EVALUATION

The recommended scheme is used to get the cost from user and suggest the best avilable server instead of configure the server and pay for its infrastructure and also user can buy a better server with the cost avilable with them. This will increase the utilization of the cloud environment especially for small business, who are not ready to spend more on IT Infrastructure cost.Cost is the biggest advantage of cloud service sometimes the same advantage will become a biggest disadvantage if not used in a proper way. Cost is biggest challenge in cloud service when we use it without proper knowlwdge.

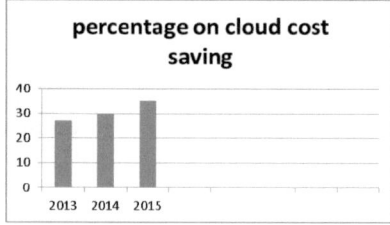

VI. CONCLUSION

With this framework user with less technical knowledge can handle the cloud server and deploy their application on cloud and also user can save cost spend on choosing cloud service for environment provisioning.

VII.REFERENCES

[1]. Trivedi,Chudasama published "Dynamic Resources Provisioning for Deadline and Budget Constrained Application in cloud Environment" in computer Technology and applications vol 4 by May-June 2013.

[2]. KC Gouda, TV Radhika, M Akshatha published "Prioirity based resource allocation model for cloud computing" in International journal for science, Engineering and technology research in 2013.

[3]. A.Rodriguez, J.Carretero, B.Bergua and F.Garcia published "Resource selection for fast large-scale virtual propagation" in IEEE symposium on computers and communication in 2009.

[4]. "open virtualization format" details from http://www.dmft.org/standards/ovf.

[5]. Dillon. T, Chen Wu, Chang E published "cloud computing: issues and challenges" in Advanced Information Networking and Applications 2010 24th IEEE International Conference on 2010.

[6]. Rafael Weingartner, Gabriel Beims, Brascher Carlos, Backer westphall published "Cloud resource management " in journal of network and computer applications 2014.

[7]. Ahushal, Ranjita and Saikat published "Generalized Resource Allocation for cloud" in proceedings of the third symposium on Cloud computing SOCC October 2012.

[8]. Yusen Li, Xueyan Tang published "On Dynamic Bin Packing for Resource Allocation in Cloud" in 26th ACM symposium on parallelism in algorithms and architectures.

[9]. R.Bradshaw, N.Desai, T.Freeman and K Keahey published "A Scalable approach to deploying and managing appliances" in proceedings of the Terra Grid Conference 2007.

4

[10]. Bhavani B and H S Guruprasad published "Resource Provisioning Techniques in Cloud Computing Environment – A Survey" in International journal for science, Engineering and technology research vol3, 2014.

[11]. J.Branke and K deb Published "Integrating user preference into evolutionary multi-objective optimization" in Knowledge Incorporation Evolutionary Computation, pp. 461-477, 2005.

[12]. A.V.Konstantinou, T.Eilam, M.Kalantar, A.A Totok.W.Amold and E.Snible published "An Architecture for virtual solution composition and deployment in infrastructure clouds" in proceedings of the 3rd International Workshop on Virtualization Technologies in Distributed Computing, 2009.

[13]. VMware "Best Practices for building virtual appliances" White paper, Nov 2007 [Online] .

[14]. VMWare "Virtual appliance marketplace, Virtual appliances, VMware appliance." [online]. http://www.vmware.com/appliances/

[15]. Openstack for VM configuration https://www.openstack.org/

[16]. T.V.Pham, H.Jamjoom, K.Jordan and Z-Y.Sahe published "A service composition framework for market-oriented high performance computing cloud" in ACM HPDC 2010.

[17]. Sean Marstona, Zhi Lia, Subhajyoti Bandyopadhyaya, published "Cloud computing – the business perspective" Decision Support System vol51, issue1 in April 2011.

[18]. V.Talwar, Q.Wu,C.Pu, W.Yan, G.Jung and D.Milojicicin published "Comparision of approaches to service deployment" in Proceedings of IEEE International Conference on Distributed Computing systems, 2005.

[19]. Ezugwu, Buhari, Junaidu published "Virtual Machine Allocation in Cloud Environment"

[20]. L.He, S.Smith, R.Willenborg and Q.Wang published "Automating deployment and activation of virtual iamges", in IBM Web Sphere Developer Technical Journal, vol 8, Aug.2007.

[21]. Pooja, Naveen Kumari Published "Performance Evaluation of Cost-Time Based Workflow Scheduling Algorithms in cloud Computing" by International Journal of Advanced Research in computer Science and software Engineering Volume3, Issue 9, September 2013.

[22]. Tran Vu Pham published "Elastic High Performance Applications – A composition Framework", on IEEE Asia-Pacific services computing conference 2011.

[23]. Keshou Wu, Lizhao Liu, Jain Lu, Weifeng Li, Gang Xie, Xiaona Tong and Yun Lin published "Research on Grid security Authentication Algorithm in cloud computing", in journal of Networks, 2011.

[24]. IonutAydanJeff published "secure control of portable images in a virtual computing utility" in proceedings of ACM workshop on virtual machine security.

[25]. Dastjerdi, Amir Vahid, Saurabh kumar Garg, Omer F. Rana and RajKumar Buyya published "cloud pick: a framework for QOS – aware and ontology – based service deployment across clouds." in software practice and experience, 2014.

[26]. Reference link : www.acm.org , www.ijcset.net , www.irdindia.in , www.ijcta.com , www.cloudbus.org .

5